Tahquamenon Area Poems

FRANCES ALATALO
AND
LORI ANDERSON
∞
Editors

ILLUSTRATED BY BILL KOLASINSKI

1991

PUBLISHED BY THE NEWBERRY NEWS,
NEWBERRY, MICHIGAN 49868

North by Choice; Tahquamenon Area Poems
Published 1991 by The Newberry News Inc., Newberry, Mich.
   49868

All rights reserved by the poets and the illustrator. No part of this book may be used or reproduced in any form or by any means without prior written permission of the authors or illustrator, except for brief quotations embodied in critical articles and reviews. For more information contact The Newberry News.

ISBN 0-9629546-0-8

Back cover photography by James G. Diem

Preface

There are poets among us. We might not have known that, but Bill Diem of The Newberry News had faith that people were writing poems here. His notice in the News brought the poems in this collection. The request was for poems that reflect "the memory of a country" centered in the Eastern Upper Peninsula.

We like to think that poetry gives us extra dimensions, views of life that we might not have noticed or we did notice and have forgotten. Our poetry can remind us of a certain specialness in a moment or a lifetime. The worlds we each carry within have infinite stories, most of which are never told. We can learn to respect those stories. This kind of writing may help to bring them to our attention.

As we struggle with the harshness of our winters and our individual and community circumstances, as we bask in the blessedness of fair weather and whatever good fortune we are favored by, it is appropriate that we have words to play with for fun and for the personal feelings of accomplishment that may accompany a particular project.

A part of the pleasure of writing is the risks we take; first putting on paper something that is our own that anyone who reads can evaluate and perhaps enjoy, perhaps not. Then there is the element of can I do this, can I get away with this or that approach, can I experiment in this way? Finally, after all the work is done there may be concerns about what people think; will they like this poem, is this a GOOD poem, am I a poet after all? We want to thank our authors who may have taken those risks and sent us these poems.

Hopefully the future will bring other poems to describe more completely the spirit of a distinctive and beautiful place.

Frances Alatalo and Lori Anderson
Newberry, Michigan

April 16, 1991

Contents

SOME HISTORY

The Whistles of the Town 2
    BILLIE J. OBEY

Charcoal Iron 4
    OSCAR SUNDSTROM

The Sawmill 4
    OSCAR SUNDSTROM

Cloverland Bakery 4
    OSCAR SUNDSTROM

Sherman's Drug Store 4
    OSCAR SUNDSTROM

Sundstrom's Store 5
    OSCAR SUNDSTROM

Horner Flooring 5
    OSCAR SUNDSTROM

Pine Stump Junction 5
    OSCAR SUNDSTROM

Century Old Lutheran Church 5
    OSCAR SUNDSTROM

Tahquamenon Falls Trip 6
    OSCAR SUNDSTROM

Saturday Night in Town 6
    OSCAR SUNDSTROM

Food Fare 6
    OSCAR SUNDSTROM

Nothing Rhymes 6
    OSCAR SUNDSTROM

A Mare Named Queen 7
    MURRAY PALMER

Logging in the U.P. 8
    N. JUNE PEAKE

Winter and Other Seasons

Welcome Snow! 12
    Trish Lasslett

Snow 13
    Robert Schaefer

Lonely? 14
    Beverly Schaefer

The Big Snow 15
    R.R. Fretz

One Day Skiing 16
    Lori Anderson

Cabin Fever 17
    N. June Peake

Jack Frost 18
    N. June Peake

Jangled Bells 19
    Dr. Peter Schaefer and Lt. Richard Schaefer

Returning Youth 20
    Lori Anderson

Northern Highways 21
    John E. Lee

Travel Woes 22
    Oscar Sundstrom

End of a Weekend 23
    Frances Alatalo

Bird of the Hour 23
    Frances Alatalo

The Gray Squirrel 24
    N. June Peake

Nature 25
    P.J. Walsh

Springtime in the U.P. 27
    SAVILLA HANDRICH

This Place 28
    FRANCES ALATALO

The Birth of Spring 30
    MURRAY PALMER

My Rainbow 31
    MARGARET JORDAN FURLONG

Maple Trees 32
    N. JUNE PEAKE

Shared Tree 33
    SPRAGUE TAYLOR

Snow on My Mind 34
    N. JUNE PEAKE

WATER, WATER ALL AROUND

Tahquamenon (1965) 38
    LINNEA HENDRICKSON

Tahquamenon, the Falls 39
    FRANCES ALATALO

Tahquamenon, the River 41
    FRANCES ALATALO

Moods of Lake Superior 43
    TRISH LASSLETT

Superior Shores 44
    MURRAY PALMER

The Agate Hunter 45
    MARY LOU BAKER

The Pond 46
    CAROL JENKINS

Glimmerglass Lake 48
    N. JUNE PEAKE

To Fish with Finn 49
    LORI ANNE ANDERSON

Shanty Fishin' 50
    P.J. WALSH

Fishing – Just for the Fun of It 51
    ROBERT SCHAEFER

HUNTING AND TRAPPING

Cedar Swamp 56
    BILL DIEM

November Madness 58
    DAVID JAY WALSH

The Deer Blind 60
    ROBERT SCHAEFER

The Buck That Got Away 62
    N. JUNE PEAKE

Grandpa's Gun 63
    FRANK GORDON

My Guide Dick 64
    FRANK GORDON

Dick Shot Her Through in '62 65
    FRANK GORDON

The Mighty Hunter 66
    M. WALSH

U.P. 67
    JOHN E. LEE

The U.P. Trapper 68
    ROBERT ONICA

A Variety of Thought

Moving to the Upper Peninsula 71
  R.R. Fretz

You and I 72
  Chas. Wheatley

Flight 73
  Nancy DeVerna

The Pictured Carpet 74
  P.J. Walsh

A Tribute to Mothers 76
  M. Walsh

The Teacher's Prayer 78
  M. Walsh

50th Wedding Anniversary 79
  M. Walsh

There's No Place Like Home 80
  R. Blanchard

A Walk in the Woods 80
  Alice Diem

Fie on Your Photo 81
  Mary Lou Baker

Riding the Dryer in the Laundromat 81
  Linnea Hendrickson

Ages Old Dilemmas

Gone Is My Eden 84
  Katheryn Kunert Bitters

A Gentle Man 85
  Trish Lasslett

Untitled 87
  Angel Messer

Emptiness 88
    LORI ANDERSON

Abandoned Fields 89
    MURRAY PALMER

Priorities 90
    FRANCES ALATALO

A Voice from Within 91
    CAROL DALE LEWIS

A Quality of Life 92
    LORI ANDERSON

The War 93
    WARREN MASON

Soldier 94
    WARREN MASON

Freedom 95
    P.J. WALSH

Conscious 96
    P.J. WALSH

Peek-A-Boo Moon 97
    TRISH LASSLETT

BIOGRAPHICAL NOTES 98

INDEX 101

Some History

It is great to be a part of a community which has natives who remember our Newberry of the old days. Many pass along with joy and nostalgia the tales told to them by settlers and loggers of earlier times. Here in the 1990s we can only experience the old times through stories and poems. Through them we can envision the old logging camps, store fronts, train depot and sounds of the past. We begin our poetry with some delightful historical notes about Newberry.

Logging has been an essential part of Newberry history. Wood charcoal fueled the iron smelter, lumber and pulp kept the town going, and wood remains a vital part of our economy today. The two poems about logging included here describe some personal details past and present.

The Whistles of the Town
By Billie J. Obey

Much has been written about our small town,
And the great virgin forests that grew all around.
The railroad men who came to lay track,
In every direction to bring the logs back
To the chemical plant and lumber mills that sprang
   up around.
But I've never heard mention, the whistles of the
   town.
Whistles blew at six o'clock, it was the start of day,
Others blew at eight o'clock to get us on our way.
Kids were bundled up real warm and hustled off to
   school
Some had to walk a good long way to learn the
   golden rule.
Because there was a railroad, trains added to the
   sound,
With their steam whistles blowing as they rushed in
   and out of town.
The passenger train came in at noon, or there about,
And it returned again at four, as school was letting
   out.
We'd hurry home to do our chores, as supper Mom
   would fix,
She'd call out, "Come in to eat," when the whistle
   blows at six.
After supper dishes were done, we'd go out to play,
Until the eight o'clock whistle signaled the end of
   our day.
We'd put on nightshirts, brush our teeth, get into
   bed, and then,
All were usually sound asleep when the whistle
   blew at ten.

There wasn't any place, from home, that you could
   stray,
Be it swimming up at High Banks or fishing Spider
   Bay,
That the whistles would not reach with their loud
   demanding bray.
To say you did not hear them, was not of any use,
If late you'd better find an iron-clad excuse.
For then, a trip to the woodshed was not considered
   abuse.
Then, as I grew older, I came to realize.
The ever blowing whistles regulated all the town
   folks' lives.
Shop doors were opened, men went to work at a
   mill,
And many, men and women, to the asylum on the
   hill.
The chemical plant worked day and night, Atlas
   Plywood too,
To keep the shifts right on time, their old steam
   whistles blew.
During this time the lumberjacks cut, and sawed
   and slashed,
The bosses did not seem concerned this product
   could not last.
So, one by one, the lumber companies were left
   empty or torn down,
And with them went, the now forgotten, Whistles of
   the Town.

Charcoal Iron
By Oscar Sundstrom

The old blast furnace would belch and smoke,
About nine p.m. they added the coke,
The 'pigs' flowed out in fierce red rows,
When the plug man shouted – "There She Blows!"

The Sawmill
By Oscar Sundstrom

The sawyer eyed each log on the deck,
The carriageman grappled with 'dogs' and 'sets',
The sixty inch circle would rip and roar,
As each plank was added to the talleyman's score.

Cloverland Bakery
By Oscar Sundstrom

Our town was famous for Cloverland bread,
This was made by baker Ed,
He fed the town, the schools, the camps,
And day old donuts to lots of tramps.

Sherman's Drug Store
By Oscar Sundstrom

Gus' Drug Store served our town,
From Lydia Pinkhams to Hadacol,
Notions, plasters, liniments too,
But his famous FLYDOPE was best of all.

Sundstrom's Store
By Oscar Sundstrom

Royal tailors, Munsingwear, shoes and spats and more,
Good drygoods, public rooms for Moms and kids galore,
Eight languages spoken here with trading to and fore,
Long ago, I've heard it said –
That was Sundstrom's Store.

Horner Flooring
By Oscar Sundstrom

Hardwood floors from Horner's mill,
Were known throughout the land,
They surpassed the toughest standards,
My, they are STILL just grand.

Pine Stump Junction
By Oscar Sundstrom

Millions of tombstone-gray old stumps,
Show us where great pines once stood,
We'll never know that awesome sight,
Don't you really wish you could?

Century Old Lutheran Church
By Oscar Sundstrom

In the 1880's those immigrants came,
They spoke mostly Finn and Swede,
They worked and saved, and churches were built,
Humbly, we honor their deed.

Tahquamenon Falls Trip
By Oscar Sundstrom

The "Betty-B" ran a daily spree,
Ol' Bucky Scott drove the trolley,
They hauled a barge with a crowd so large,
The full day's trip was jolly –
Son-of-a-gun– it was FUN!

Saturday Night in Town
By Oscar Sundstrom

The 'jacks came in droves back when pine was
    king,
Two nights in town was a mighty fling,
Johnson's, Larson's and Mammies too,
Food, drinks and cavorting was everyone's due.

Food Fare
By Oscar Sundstrom

My OH my- how continental-
Mignon with quiche and sushi too,
Lots of folks have long forgotten
Rabbit hash and mulligan stew.

Nothing Rhymes
By Oscar Sundstrom

Inevitably there comes a time
When thoughts crop up in great disorder,
No matter what we try to rhyme,
Nothing fits the second line.

A Mare Named Queen
By Murray Palmer

A dog they say is a man's best friend,
    And for most I would agree.
But a sorrel mare by the name of Queen
    Was more than a friend to me.

I loved that old mare, and I always will.
    And rarely a day goes by,
Should I reminisce and think of our past,
    You may find a tear in my eye.

In rain or snow, in heat or sleet,
    Old Queen was always there.
I've known of some who did well too,
    But few with her compared.

I've seen her work knee deep in snow,
    And struggle knee deep in muck.
But I never saw her tire and quit.
    Whatever the job, she stuck.

With reins tied high on the horns of her hames,
    I would turn her loose on her own.
I loved to show how well she could skid,
    When she worked by my voice alone.

She knew the meaning of gee and haw.
    And responded, at once, to whoa.
For she knew me, as I knew her,
    And she knew not a cuss or a blow.

It seemed as though we were as one,
    We did our work so well,
That many a sawyer would stop to watch.
    She seemed to weave a spell.

The age of the horse in the woods is past,
    And so is my old mare Queen.
But in a sense she will always live.
    In my heart and in my dreams.

Logging in the U.P.
By N. June Peake

The logging in the U.P.
Is not a thing of the past
But if we don't replant the forest
How long will it last

Roads to make, stumps to move
Timber to be marked
Must get on with the skidding
Can't leave the machinery parked

Four foot logs, eight foot logs
The sawyers are doing well
Lots of timber in this stand
Many logs to fell

Truckloads to haul to sidings
Railroad cars waiting there
This might go to Baker's in G.R.
To make a beautiful chair

Roads drift full and then we wait
The plows are on their way
We've got to get the logs in
So the men can get their pay

Cables that snap, tires that blow
On guard we'll always be
'Cause if there's a widow maker
I don't want it to get me

We build a small warm fire
To heat our frozen lunch
Then it's back to work in the snow
Where our footsteps they do crunch

Saws abuzzing, canthooks flying
Our quota we must fill
So keep the logs amoving to
Get them to the mill

Winter and Other Seasons

Among the many blessings of living in the Upper Peninsula is the opportunity to fully experience the changing seasons.

To some of us it seems that we have only two seasons: winter and a brief interlude before the next winter. Some say that we have only two temperatures here in the North: cold and very cold. Our winters get to feeling long and lonely. Frozen highways and bitter winds keep some close to home. The adventurers take to snowmobiling, skiing, ice fishing and other winter sports. Our homes never felt as cozy as after braving a winter storm to work or play.

Friends seem dearer, enjoying each other's company, coffee mug in hand, while outside snow blows in the wind. Social events and school sports keep many people busy regardless of the season.

Our authors have chosen many topics representative of the area. The most numerous concern winter, cold and snow. Having to spend a lot of time at home is a good setup for thinking and writing if one is so inclined.

Spring does finally come after many fits and starts. Each fair day and even rainy ones are filled with industry and activity as well as singing birds and smiling faces. Storm windows come down and laundry hangs on the line again. Children are dirty from playing outside. Gardeners prepare whatever they can. Summer in the U.P. can be glorious and it seems all too short. Perhaps that is why we have no poems specifically about summer. There are so many things to do outside, pens and pencils get left at home.

Perhaps autumn has the same pattern. We hurry to finish projects and prepare for winter. As one of our authors puts it, "snow is on my mind."

Welcome Snow!
By Trish Lasslett

White pillows nesting on pine boughs
Puffy white wedges caught in tree branches
White fields lay undisturbed
Smiling faces looking out the windowpane
Anticipation of a new snowman
Mittens, hats, scarves and boots
Join together with a snowsuit
To welcome a new, fresh fallen snow
Covering the world in a blanket of white
We welcome you new snow
For you make the world beautiful and bright.

Snow
By Robert Schaefer

Snow is neat and pretty and fluffy and white;
If you fall in it, your injuries are slight!

Snow piles up in drifts and ridges and bumps;
It covers grass and weeds, old cars and stumps.

Snow makes snowmen and forts and on it you can ski;
It makes snowballs you can throw at teachers, kids you don't like and me!

Snow is frigid and wet and biting cold;
It can chill you or challenge you whether young or old.

Snow is deep and steep and one of my most favorite things;
It pleases me and teases me and cheers me, except when it comes in the spring!

Lonely?
By Beverly Schaefer

When morning comes and I look out
Into a world so calm and white
Visitors have left their signs
As they came here in the dark last night.

The deer who made them long since gone
Betrayed by tracks left in the snow
(and monkey tracks and bear tracks, too.
So Robert says, and he should know!)

A mink showed up, down on the ice
He stayed a moment – then slipped below
into the water – oh how cold –
I watched him and I saw him go.

The feeder is a busy place
With constant flight of chickadees
As busily they eat the seeds.
And other birds come from the trees

A goldfinch in his winter's drab,
The nuthatch quick – the squawking jay.
And sometimes, too, a frisky squirrel
Onto the feeder finds his way.

When people ask with kind intent
If I do not feel "housebound."
I can answer "No, indeed.
Not with all this life around!"

The Big Snow
By R.R. Fretz

Snow, like people, comes
in all shapes and sizes.
It covers the North
in numerous guises.
Sometimes it's small, like
God gave us a dusting.
It leaves skiers and
Sledders hoping, lusting.
They seek a deep base
But often, it's just slush.
When warm weather comes
Drifts become molten mush.
My favorite snow
Falls fast, heavily heaped
Hills mound by the foot
While kids create a keep.
I enjoy the trees,
Especially a pine
Delicately draped,
Winter is at its prime.
Pure blinding white snow
Shining so crystal clear
Pouring from the clouds
Yes, it's my time of year.

One Day Skiing
By Lori Anne Anderson

If I could write these
    sounds I hear
I'd write a song all
    souls would know.

Wind so slight through
    trees now bare
a breeze of comfort soft,
    light and fair.

Faint calls like echoes
    alone and far
a gift to me – I wish
    to hear.

A song so sweet my heart
    does start
and looks to see what
    calls me here.

Are they aware this heart
    they stir?
sweet sigh and song for
    my content?

Fair song of bird and
    sigh of wind
a harmonious tune for
    all akin.

CABIN FEVER
By N. June Peake

Cooped up for days on end
The weather was a fright
Mr. Sunshine couldn't be found
He was nowhere in sight

It would last forever
Snow clouds everywhere
Wouldn't some one stop by
But no one seemed to care

One day I felt the warmth
Was that dripping eaves I heard
Was that noise that I detected
The chirping of a bird

The fever raged on and on
With no relief in sight
Then I realized it was Cabin Fever
And I knew I'd be all right

Jack Frost
By N. June Peake

Have you ever been alone
For days on end
With not a soul to talk to
Not one single friend

The flurries just keep coming
The roads are drifted full
No one coming or going
No children on sleds to pull

The storm clouds are gathering
Not a single sunshine ray
Won't someone come and ask me
Can you come out to play?

I sat alone by the window
And seemed to feel so lost
Then along came my winter visitor
It was old Jack Frost

Jack made designs on my window
Frost was here to stay
He beckoned unto me and said
Come on out and play

We made a snowman with a hat
And angels in the snow
My friend is here to stay 'til spring
Let the cold wind blow.

Jangled Bells
By Dr. Peter Schaefer and Lt. Richard Schaefer

Dashing through da snow, in da wife's new snow
    machine,
Run into a stump, ya should ah heard her scream.
She flew right over my head, into da cedar tree,
When she finally got back to da ground,
She come right after me.

Jangled bells, jangled bells, the wife she's mad at
    me
Ever since we hit dat stump, and flew into dat tree
Machine don't run, she bought a gun, she's really
    sore at me
I suppose dat she won't never forget
Da time she kissed dat tree.

Returning Youth
By Lori Anne Anderson

The smells of the changing season
set my soul to fly away.
I'm bursting from my body
inside, I cannot stay.

I feel a rush of memories
as the winter smell sets in.
Consumed with such emotion
I wonder where I am.

I shut my eyes and
use my senses
breathing in each
brisk cold fragrance.

And my mind slips back
ten years in time to
snowman statues and
fairy tale rhymes.

Northern Highways
By John E. Lee

The northern highways are seldom clear;
Their ice and snow can bring on fear.

There are miles and miles of nothing but trees.
It's an awesome sight that can bring you to your knees.

The wind blows hard, the snow sails along.
It howls in your ears as it sings you a song

Of nature – of danger – of things yet to come;
Of things that will chill you and make you feel numb.

The hum of your motor makes you feel good –
That blessed heat from under your hood.

Your wipers your radio fill you with cheer.
You're hoping that soon a town will appear.

You're watching the road – in your eyes there's a strain.
Your head begins to hurt – there's a genuine pain.

Way down in the highway you see something there.
Is it an oncoming car or maybe a bear?

It keeps coming closer you think it's a car;
It's still hard to tell – it still is so far.

Yes, it's a car and it's coming quite fast,
With a swish of the air and now it is past.

The great cloud of snow it leaves in its wake
Totally blinds you – you must touch the brake.

You touch it real easy – you don't want to slide.
If you sailed off the road with trees you'd collide.

Traveling these roads is a real scary thing –
The ice and the snow and all that winter brings.

So put on your belt and don't drive fast;
If cars are in a hurry let them go past.

To get where you're going is your main goal,
Not to have a wreck and be stuck in the cold.

Travel Woes
By Oscar Sundstrom

Little drops of water
Little flakes of snow
Make the super highways
Pretty doggone slow.

END OF A WEEKEND
By Frances Alatalo

Sunday night
cars are
all headed south
their trailers
with snowmobiles
in twos and fours
whizzing along
behind.
The long trail
of lights moves
like a
live dragon
miles long
scaly sides
flashing
reflecting
occasional
smoke
steam
snow
flying up.

BIRD OF THE HOUR
By Frances Alatalo

A small bedraggled chickadee
Out there alone amazes me
He is this blizzard's certain hero
Singing in temperatures far under zero.

The Gray Squirrel
By N. June Peake

Outside my kitchen window
The fat gray squirrel sits
In a knothole in a big tree
She thinks winter is the pits.

She peeks into my window
To see if I am up
And finds me staring groggily
Into my coffee cup.

I've saved some peanuts for her
She gets a few each day
And she clamors down to get them
In the midst of morning play.

She sits on her haunches
Nibbling from both paws
She must be wary of the hawks
They have very sharp claws.

She travels to the neighbors
On a round electric cord
Pretends that she's a Walenda
Never getting bored.

Tummy full and playtime over
She returns for a rest
The thoughtful look upon her face
Says she likes summers best.

Nature
By P.J. Walsh

Nature, how grand you are!
You ramble on and on so far.

You give us snow with all its beauty,
Then Jack Frost, who does his duty.

The sun, it seems so far away,
And then the moon, he has full sway.

But later on the days get long,
The birds of Spring then sing their song.

The rush of waters on their way,
Lure spawning fish in April or May.

The bark of maples seldom bleed,
Best maple syrup is guaranteed!

The buds of leaves come on the trees,
And this is sure to end the freeze.

The farmer then can plant his grain,
And with the seeds, he'll pray for rain.

Trailing arbutus can then be found,
If time is taken to look around.

In hardwoods bloom the lilies fair,
When springtime blends with summer's air;

And southern breeze is all around,
Much consolation then is found.

But harvest time, it comes so soon

And with it comes the Autumn moon.

Then migratory birds fly south
The old shotgun comes off the shelf.

The spuds are taken from the ground
And stored away in one big mound.

We find the time is near at hand
To cut our need for winter grand

The leaves of Autumn flutter in the breeze
As we hunt the partridge in the trees.

November gives us deer and bear
When Thanksgiving seems to fill the air.

Of course December brings us snow
Then old Winter's here again, you know.

We truly thank you, Nature, is our intention
"Continue on; forgive the things we didn't
    mention."

April 12, 1943

Springtime in the U.P.
By Savilla Handrich

The bright colored tulips are doing their thing
Fat clumsy robins fly by on wing
Making our world glow and sing
Our U.P. of Michigan, in the beautiful spring!

Budding and green, beautiful trees
Streams, rocks, rivers, and lakes, if you please
Deer with their fawns, and bunnies that sneeze
Tall graceful cattails that sway in the breeze.

Beaver that duck, partridge that hide
Warm breezes now that long were denied
Friends that stroll up main street and side
Make this a great little place to reside.

Marsh marigold grow in bright golden hue
Gander and goose walking two by two
Followed by goslings, fluffy and new
I've seen it all, and it's true, it's true!!

One thing however, of which I can't boast
The "black fly" makes me, a reluctant host
Can't chase 'em, can't swat 'em, can't hit 'em with
    a post
Thank God, they stay two weeks at the most.

THIS PLACE
BY FRANCES ALATALO

It's that the cold
makes me alert
to any shelter
even those
the mind contrives.
It's that life
is not easy
in the North
you must constantly
use your wits
or muscle and
so develop
admire support
make your own
small environments
ignoring hazards.
It's that I
have lain
on sunny beaches
and watched
the huge moon
of the South
and got concerned
with fripperies
instead of life's
swift advance.
It's that spring
in the North
is more like
a miracle
following winter
the blossoms

seem not possible
the sun melts
dispositions
life glitters
away the
daily discords
brief truces
nature's restoratives
feeding on
the frigid freezing
warm melting
light darkness
of this place.

The Birth of Spring
By Murray Palmer

Listen to the axes ring,
hear the song they seem to sing.
The tempo's fast, the beat is strong,
It picks you up, then sweeps along.

Listen to the axes ring,
Watch the woodsman as he swings.
See the chips fly through the air,
His strike is bold as if a dare.

Listen to the axes ring,
Heralding the birth of spring.
A winter full we leave behind,
The spring that comes brings peace of mind.

My Rainbow
By Margaret Jordan Furlong

When I wash my clothes
And they are hung to dry
I like to watch them
Waving on the line.
A potpourri of things so bright,
From snowy whites to pink and azure blue
Lilac, too, and flaming red,
A rainbow true –
All mine, upon the line.

*Submitted by her daughter,
Margaret Furlong DeChant*

Maple Trees
By N. June Peake

The maples of the U.P.
Are a sight to behold
Tall and gracefully standing
With colors that are bold

The greens of the summer
Turning yellow, orange, and red
Their reflections in the water
Of streams that are spring fed

The northwinds come ablowing
Carrying leaves gently to the ground
We laugh and walk among them
Making a loud swishing sound

We rake them into piles
The winds scatter them anew
The frost is on the pumpkins
The leaves are covered with dew

The bare trees now seem lonesome
Making eerie shadows on the ground
We watch them until springtime
When with new buds they'll abound

Shared Tree
By Sprague Taylor (1920 - 1976)

I pulled down fruit from an apple tree
That a bear had visited before.
Alone, in a small clearing, age
Has brought the tree to such pilferage

As we commit each fall, and hours apart
From each other, to give each other search;
I in the high, easily broken limbs that start
Beyond his snuffling at his bear's-high reach.

We leave our several signs and smells
Of foraging, both high and low
When the day is mine, and nighttime tells
Of his emergence from the swamp below.

But no deterrent keeps us back
From the lure of that apple tree;
He gorging, I with a peck-size sack
In our last, pre-hibernal spree.

Submitted by Carol Taylor

Snow on My Mind
By N. June Peake

The leaves are now a brilliant hue
The snow is not far behind
It's all I think about lately
It's always on my mind

Gone are the summer flowers
Of every color and kind
The blanket of snow is coming
It's always on my mind

No more trips to Round Lake
Where on picnics we all dined
Now it's shovels, boots, and mittens
Snow is always on my mind

Faucets to drain, bushes to mulch
I don't dare fall behind
The northern wind is blowing
And snow is on my mind

Soon the deer will be herding
Their food will be hard to find
Beautiful "white stuff" will cover it
There is snow on my mind

A cozy fire in the fireplace
For the robins we all pined
As we sat and shared our memories
There was snow on my mind

WATER, WATER ALL AROUND

Water, Water All Around

Tourists and natives alike flock to the lakes and streams in our area. Tahquamenon Falls is probably most popular with tourists. Close to it is Lake Superior and Whitefish Point with the Shipwreck Museum, agate hunters and bird watchers. Many other lakes, rivers, ponds and swamps provide recreation, nature study and occupation. A variety of fishing and swimming holes and scenic beaches are always enjoyed. The power and energy in many of these waters is tremendous. We may be elated as we stand and ponder the magnificence of that power, but we are saddened when lives are lost in the waters. The Tahquamenon River, Lake Superior and the Two-Hearted River have been an inspiration to writers of the past. Our authors have also been inspired by the waters that surround us. Experiencing so much water, it is difficult to imagine a drought or rationed water.

Tahquamenon (1965)
By Linnea Hendrickson

Strewing their Kodapak boxes
Shoving their babies in strollers,
Slapping mosquitoes and eating Drumsticks
In Hiawatha's woodland,
The tourists come to see the falls.

I leave them behind,
Lured by the power of roaring lace and
Whirlwind sting of spray behind the veil.
A mosquito beneath an upraised hand
I stand, daring the trembling overhang
To fall, or let drop a rock like those that fell
A million years ago or yesterday.
For a moment we are one:
The water, the rock, the roar,
The tourists, the mosquito, and me,
A second and a million years.

Cold and sunshine greet me as I scurry
Out from concave cliffs on slippery clay.

Tahquamenon, the Falls
By Frances Alatalo

Recently we visited Tahquamenon, the Falls
It was a lovely day, the kind that calls
you out of doors so it was crowded
on the steps and landings all about it.
There were people taking pictures
subjects standing tall,
and standing close were people
surveying overall.
People hypnotized by water rushing brown
shiny looking water slipping swiftly down.
Water, water all around going by so quickly
you felt as if you're moving too
a feeling somewhat sickly.
But everyone was happy
you could tell their walk was snappy.
Some exclaimed and some were quiet
but it's sure that most would certify it
was the highlight of their trip.
As parents admonished children not to slip
husbands waited, wives were talking
almost everyone was walking
snapping pictures of the water falling down.

A young boy said "It's awesome."
A toddler cried because some
popcorn fell into the water floating down.
We all watched it looking very white
the water very brown
the slippery shiny water rushing down.
Immediately the popcorn disappeared
into the bottom really down.
Imagining it was fearful

but the child no longer tearful
pointed to the spot with solemn
and investigative face
then smiled at all of us
as though enchanted with the place.

Then back up the steps we started
and the generations parted,
children running up and elders slow behind.
There we counted as we mounted
just to see how many steps we'd find.
One said eighty-nine and then some more
Maybe it was ninety-four.
On the trail above we walked on
joined the others, some had gone.
"To the bottom," children shouted.
Some agreed and others pouted.
Steps and more steps, landings too.
we went up and down a few.
Someone said two hundred
steps but who can count
with such a view?

So we lingered while the light changed
And we pondered as the colors ranged
from light to dark and back again all brown
and the moving water told us
that of all the things that mold us
nature surely has advantage over town.
Then we knew that we'd return
to this place where waters churn
where the shiny slippery water
spills it's fancy overload,
where we felt rejuvenated
as we headed down the road.

TAHQUAMENON, THE RIVER
By Frances Alatalo

It starts out
in an empty
wild place,
I've heard,
Some know
just where that is.
One day perhaps
I'll stand there
thinking baby talk
beginnings
and "Dr. Livingston,
I presume."
Our river runs
through swamp and bog
Tamarack forest
plastered green
up to the Falls
which most of us
have seen,
then onward
to Superior,
Rivermouth
and traffic.
The bends
and swirls
of this
short silken stream
have been known
to many –
men, women, children.
Their adventures
could fill

a thousand books.
Instead
these amazing stories
have run down
to Lake Superior
where they joke
and dance
in the sparkling waves,
camouflage currents
and howl with the winds.
Sometimes
standing near
we hear them.

Moods of Lake Superior
By Trish Lasslett

Rushing, Tumbling, Rolling,
Blowing, Breaking, Smashing,
Gray, Dark, Threatening,
Quiet, Slowing,
Still, Smooth, Gentle,
Blue, Bright, Soothing,
Gently Waving, Beckoning . . .

Superior Shores
By Murray Palmer

The ocean beat against the shore,
And spent itself on stone.
Which glistened from this sweet caress
As though they basked in love.

Each dashing wave embraced the shore,
And sent its spray in air,
That bore a beat of primal joy,
And there were ears to hear.

The tempo was a steady throb,
A most contagious song.
Which brought all hearers to the scene,
Then lulled them deep and strong.

Throughout the noon and all the night
The sea pursued its court.
But come the dawn its passion spent,
It lay at peace in calm.

What made this aged titan deep
Seek out these granite stone?
Which lie alone in frigid air
Now that they lie alone.

It seemed as though they were as one
When storm was at its height.
But now they make a sorry pair,
And not the least alike.

The Agate Hunter
By Mary Lou Baker

Lone figure, hooded, booted,
Leans against the wild wind-spray,
Glories in the flood of sea waves
Flinging rocks onto the shore,
Washing banks into the maelstrom,
Grinding with tumultuous roar.

Eyes detect the gleam of color,
Line of pattern, sought-for prize.
Hands caress the wondrous gemstone,
Marvel at its swirling form;
Spirits soar at earth's rewarding
Challenge to Superior's storm.

Whence your source, O jeweled beauty?
Lava from a violent past,
In the distant northern regions
Turned to sea, where bubbles filled,
Like pearl-culture in reverse,
By the layer, this treasure built.

Later came the mighty glacier
With its monumental force,
Carried rock and sea-life fossils,
Scooped and scraped the mounds and meres,
Dumped its load in melting puddles,
There to lie ten thousand years.

So earth's cataclysmic power
And patient eons in repose
Fashioned brilliants in the darkness,
Only now the splendor cast
Before the seeker on the shoreline
In his neverending quest.

The Pond
By Carol Jenkins

The white thick crust of ice and snow
keeps my face from the hot sun.
The robins are here with the snowbirds
believing the season of spring.
Still, my covering lingers across me
with only a crack to show the beginning
of a change.

The sun is setting . . . capturing the
shadows of the tall pines and casting
them across the white and sparkling
silver – the winter cover God gives me.

I have many memories of the past – the
children fishing in me when weather is warm.
The boys with the BB guns ending the frog's
life to put a treat on the table for their
family. The dogs dashing in and out of me
to cool from the heat, or just playing in
my weeds and cattails.
Some cars go by throwing their discards into
me – my bottom is lined with the old and
needless. Most respect me, but a few are
thoughtless.

Ducks have landed on me in route both North and
South – usually overnighters.
Beavers have indeed made their homes here,
clearing and gnawing large trees in half – building
their dams and having their young.
The river they used to travel through is dried up
now – but its deep ridge is tunneled in the ground,
marking the past.

In winters past when conditions were right and not
too much snow fell but cold prevailed, I entertained
the local folks who built their fire along
my side – roasted their dinners, sang and watched
those enjoying my clear crust to their skating
      enjoyment.
Old timers reminiscing, children clearing a hockey
area and those sliding down my banks on the clear
crystal that God painted that winter.

I have been left mainly untouched by any changes
the world may bring to other areas. I still wait
for the buds on the trees to spring forth and all
the excitement that comes with the spring and
      God's
little creatures, be they animal or human. I am
still here for all to enjoy, whether to sit by and
calm the nerves, reflect on the beauty of all around
me, or animals just stopping to drink from my
      wealth
and I am waiting now for the change – but God is
      slow
to unwrap me this year (He has his reasons) and I
      will
wait and enjoy this overcoat I wear – a little longer,
as things will change . . . they always do.

Glimmerglass Lake
(Hulbert Lake)
By N. June Peake

The sun was up, the breeze was slight
The roostertail followed in our wake
We had come for a day of fishing
On beautiful Glimmerglass Lake

There'd be perch aplenty
With sun spreading shiny rays
In just a matter of minutes
It would burn off the haze

The white birch stood tall along the shore
I was awed at the beautiful sight
A shore lunch had been packed
We'd stay 'til the moon rose up at night

There was the boys' private swimming hole
At the far end of the Lake
A stretch of sand at Sandy Beach
Where our picnics we did take

Another place called Little Rock
But the stone it was immense
You could swim out to the raft
If you used your common sense

The raft was built of barrels and wood
With carpeting no less
And we didn't have to worry
About the monster of Loch Ness

A fire for roasting hot dogs
We sang our school song
Farewell parties were held there
Has it really been that long

To Fish with Finn
By Lori Anne Anderson

Sleep burdened I pull myself
down the stairs.
The smell of coffee wakes
my tired senses.

And him, up since dawn,
alert and quick.
His eyes infinite blue tell
 me a tale
of a rugged decent man,
a stormy soul.
A morning warm and easy
we set off.

A forlorn Superior morn we
arrive alone.
South wind greets us newly.
Cheeks blush cold.

Casting far away and deep
dark, we wait.
His calloused fingers
cast a spell
and play a magic trick
or trade? We
fish a day and half a night,
not a bite.

Instead we ponder land and
lake and . . . why?
Holding dear our sameness in
this marvel here.

Ah, a bridge between our souls.

Shanty Fishin'
By P. J. Walsh

Spearin' season's here again
    It's January 1st you see,
Nature callin' all fishermen
    For sixty days of grand melee.

We buy our license first of all
    And out the shanty goes,
We think of that first pike to fall
    With fever ever in our toes

Sittin' in the old fish shanty
    All so cozy and so warm,
Thinkin' of a great big dandy
    Worryin' none about the storm.

We place our shanty on the spot
    And fire up the little stove,
Then drop that decoy like a shot
    It's time to watch for pike by jove!

Some folks do not understand
    Why we have so much fun,
They never even try their hand
    At takin' Northern on the run.

But if they try this little game
    They're sure to change their mind
They may become a little lame
    But many pleasure thrills they'll find.

Whenever spare time comes along
    Just try us Sportsmen's fun,
To work and work is sometimes wrong
    When so much fishin's to be done.

January 30, 1943

Fishing – Just for the Fun of It
By Robert Schaefer

I built a shanty 4 x 6
Covered with plywood and a frame of sticks.
A door in the front and a hole in the floor,
Stools in two corners, who could ask for more?

I sit in the dark, and stare down a hole,
If I didn't know better, I'd think I'm a mole.
The fish come by every once in a while,
And when I pull one up it brings on a smile.

The stove gets too hot, the flame may blow out;
I'm having a ball, of that there's no doubt.
My neck is getting stiff, my back is in pain;
If I last out the day, I'll surely have to strain.

My line is in tangles, the bait needs a change;
I think it's about time for me to rearrange.
That last perch I caught was about 4 inches long,
I'm feeling so happy, I burst out in song.

Hours go by, not a fish is in sight;
Though it's sunny outside, inside it's like night.
My mind has gone numb as I sit there and stare,
I think I'll step outside and get some fresh air.

I'm having a great time, it's all very fun;
It's better than Florida, lying in the sun.
You don't get sunburned, or eaten by a shark;
You set in the shanty by yourself in the dark.

I'm starting to get bored, the fish are on strike;
I can't catch a thing, and that's not really right!

The fish should start biting in a hour or so,
If I could just catch one big one to store in the
    snow.

But, I'm having a real good time,
Of that there's little doubt.
It's getting late in the day,
My time is about to run out.

I got a kink in my back,
A sprain in my neck.
What's so important about catching a fish;
Is it worth making me a wreck?

I'll tell you my friends,
If you want to have fun;
Go fishing with me in winter,
You never get done.

HUNTING AND TRAPPING

Hunting and Trapping

Hunting and trapping are main pursuits of many residents and visitors. What started as a necessity for survival in earlier days has become a skilled avocation for men and women alike. Going to Deer Camp has become as meticulously planned and anticipated as Christmas Day is for a child. Many special events take place every year during hunting season. Trapping is also a skill of the old days, kept alive by the abundance of wildlife in our area. The hunting and trapping poems describe experiences, give advice and try to tell why these activities make for such a treasured time for these people.

CEDAR SWAMP
By Bill Diem

In a silent sea of cedar
    on the edge of Black Creek Swamp
Swims a yellow-gold retriever:
      George's Jake out on a romp.
        The trailing man lacks breath to mutter
        Though his heart shouts "Slam Bam Flutter."

Above, the snowflakes fly toward town
    To seek and find each tiny crack;
Below, they filter gently down
    To fill with fluff each creature's track.
      Without, the raging winter storm;
      Within, their breath floats moist and warm.

And inside further still, in heart
    of man and dog, comes forth a yen
To stalk for game each lovely part
    Of swamp between the church and glen.
      For dog, a natural canine surge,
      For man, a base or basic urge.

Dog, the barrel-chested bucker,
    Built to heave and haul and stack
The railroad ties that once were cut here
    For the short-lived pine-haul track.
      Now it's buck and lunge and lurch,
      Breaking trail 'round fallen birch.

Man, the city-slickered poodle,
    But with mem'ries in his veins

That show up in his office doodles –
    Lonely campfires, broken chains.
      Now he's free to chase the hare:
      Two quiet chums with quest to share.

Resting in a twisted tangle,
    Pistol cocked, he strains to hear –
Moving toward him at an angle,
    Northern trophy, Whitetail deer!
      Season closed some weeks ago;
      He knows who will eat it, though.

Snow-rimed muzzle, broadside pose,
    The deer's brown eyes scan man's of blue
Head shot? Dead shot? No one knows.
    A gun half-raised is half-down too.
      The deer bounds off, the dog bounds in
      A scene that he won't see again.

The dog must leap to bare his eyes
    As hunting pair push home through snow;
On man it pulls on tiring thighs,
    Sifts down his neck, sets cheeks aglow.
      Ahead, the hearth and burning log;
      Behind, the silent cedar bog.

November Madness
By David Jay Walsh

Come November weather changes,
Flurries white and Arctic cold,
Redcoats thinking northward ranges,
Of big-racked bucks in wooded fold.

Off brown-stained racks guns are lifted,
Dusted, sighted, cleaned, and oiled,
Spirits now cannot be shaken,
Pre-laid plans cannot be foiled.

First the license, then supplies,
had rung up quite a bill,
Yet spending could be justified,
By bringing home a kill.

Northward bound, the laden campers,
Drone on studded wheels,
Excitement mounts and nothing hampers,
Jokes and puns, laughs and squeals.

Journey's over, camp is set,
Next the tin can meal,
'Round roaring fire hunters bet,
While curious bucks size up the deal.

Morning comes and still it's dark,
When hunters eat and run,
To find a stump or pre-planned mark,
From which they'll have their fun.

Through bloodshot eyes they gaze and blink,
While waiting for their prey,
With dripping nose it's cold they think,
And long for end of day.

Noises strange invade their ears,
Their hearts begin to pump,
A hound, a crow, a squirrel, a goose,
Can bring them off their stump!

Numb with cold they walk away,
From sacred hunting spot,
Returning later in the day,
Finding clawprints fresh and hot!

Curse the luck, they fume and stew,
If only we had stayed,
Most certainly a buck or two,
Could have been displayed!

Back in camp each shares his story,
While thawing out his toes,
Of sounds and tracks and would be glory
Of elusive bucks and fearless does.

The Deer Blind
By Robert Schaefer

Sitting in a deer blind,
For hours, both morning and night;
Is an experience shared by hunters,
Who probably aren't too bright.

You carry apples and corn to feed the deer.
You carry it in by dark.
You stare at the same scenery hour by hour,
The view can be quite stark.

You fantasize about the record buck,
The biggest ever shot;
Instead you're lucky to see a doe,
And it's probably a little snot.

You feed those ungrateful buggers,
About ten bushels of corn.
You break your back carrying it in;
For your efforts, the deer give you scorn.

When a hunter tells you he's communing with
    nature,
While sitting in the blind;
Just call him a liar – in so many words,
Cause he's freezing his tired behind.

To top it off, and another thing,
The wind is always wrong.
The deer will smell you, as hunters will tell you;
Before you're there very long.

So dear friends, just listen to me;

And my sad tale of the blind.
Don't take up a sport of any sort,
And avoid punishing your behind!

Stay home with your wife and children.
Read books and watch T.V.,
Don't go to the woods to hunt the deer;
The meat you get won't be free.

In the end, the deer will outsmart you;
Coming to feed when you aren't there.
So, stay away, both night and day;
Tell folks you really don't care!

The Buck That Got Away
By N. June Peake

The blind was built
The apples were strewn
I had sat there so long
It was almost noon

I heard a branch snap
And looked up to find
It was just another hunter
Not a deer near my blind

We exchanged some pleasantries
And passed the time away
The "white tails" had eluded us
This was not to be our day

Back again at the crack of dawn
To try again my luck
The day went by and I got cold
But I didn't get my buck

The season was soon over
My aim had gotten dim
Instead of the deer feeding me
I'll be feeding him!

Grandpa's Gun
By Frank Gordon

From the blind on the back forty Dick was hunting
    that day
His luck was bad so into the woods he stalked his
    prey.
He had not gone far and stopped right short,
It was no mistake, he heard an old buck snort.

The sound of a fight came to his ear.
A real buck fight without any fears.
The bush was cracking, the sound was a din,
Dick says to himself, "I'll sneak up on him."

It was then, in the evening's dim light
Those four big horns came into sight.
Straight to his shoulder came Grandpa's gun;
He squeezed her off before he could run.

The buck went down with a mighty, ugh!
When Dick drove home that 12-gauge slug.
It was late and dark when Dick came in,
The heart on a stick and Dick with a grin.

"I got him, Dad, with the old 12-gauge."
Grandpa's gun is still the rage.

My Guide Dick
By Frank Gordon

We are out to slay the wild buck I told my boys that day,
This new fallen snow will tell us just where the buck will stray.
We had searched the whole day through
But nothing but some deer tracks to put in our stew.

Dick said, "Dad, you need a guide,
I'll take you to where the old buck hides."
We crossed the marsh and up the hill.
We took it easy and were really still.

"This is the trail," Dick said to me.
"Take a left just through the trees.
We will go to the south and drive the buck.
You are sure to see him and change your luck."
The boys had just left and I made a stop.
It was then that I heard his clippety-clop.

His head was low but his rack I saw.
My 30-30 was quick on the draw.
A shot rang out, he dropped in his tracks,
And I could see his eight-point rack.

My guide was back, close to my side,
"Dad, he's a beauty," Dick said with pride.
It will get you an honor badge from "Field and Stream."
So this is the rack I see in my dreams.

Dick Shot Her Through in '62
By Frank Gordon

It was up at Carole's and Wally's
Close to Foster City way
Where Dick and Harry went a hunting
On that first deer season day.

The buck was running up the hill
And Dick he says "I'll make him spill."
He drew a bead with his ol' "8" bore
And squeezed her off with a blast and roar.

The echo it rang from hill to hill
The buck didn't stop, he's running still.
The shot lies spent upon the ground.
The tree is split from the lead so round.

Then Dickie looked both far and near
To see if he nicked one of Wally's steers.
A sigh of relief, you can bet
When the cow stood up and was alive yet.

The night it too was bright and gay
On that first deer season day.
A supper at the church was great
A dance at Hardwood, rather late.

Harry and Pete, they too had a frown
When they shot a buck that didn't stay down.
He ran through a field and by the road passed out
When along came a car and dressed him out.

The buck with his rack is gone and free
I'm sure he's as happy as he can be
But Dick is mad as you can see
Because all he hit was an ironwood tree.

The Mighty Hunter
By M. Walsh

The Mighty Hunter great is he
Braves the cold, snow and rain.
November is the time you see
That he shall bear his pain.

He dresses warm, sits on a stump
From dawn 'til setting sun.
His wife thinks he is crazy
But he is having fun.

His hopes are high that he will get
A buck to brag about,
But if he can't then to his wife
He will have to pout.

He walks and walks into the woods
And thinks he's all alone,
But then another hunter coughs
And he begins to moan.

Suddenly before his eyes
A buck! His dream come true!
His heart beat fast – he missed the deer,
And he was very blue.

It's late at night when he gets home
So tired, cold and calm,
His dear little wife puts on the chow
And gets the analgesic balm.

This is only part of it
The rest you'll never know
Until you go what he goes thru –
The Upper Michigan cold and snow.

Now if the Season's ended
and there's no venison to fill his dish,
He'll have to brave the winter storms
And try to catch some fish.

U.P.
By John E. Lee

A U.P. camp is the place to be;
For two short weeks it's home to me.

When I first open the door and look around,
I'm greeted by dust and flies abound.

I begin to clean up – hard work for sure;
But it makes me feel good – it's part of the cure.

Back to the basics in a one room camp.
The floors are cold and the walls are damp.

But it doesn't take long with a cozy fire
To become the place I love and admire.

I lay on the bed and in my mind's eye
The walls speak to me of times gone by.

Of people from the past – of deep cold snow;
Of icy air – of wind that would blow.

Of trappers that came from working their line
Who felt the comfort that now was mine.

Of breakfast cooking that wonderful smell.
Inside was heaven outside was hell.

But no worry now the camp is here
Filled with comforts – the smells, the cheer.

A U.P. camp is the place to be.
It was good for them and it's good for me.

I love the time that I spend here
Eating good food and drinking a beer.

Being with friends or being alone,
Camp is different – yes it's different than home.

The U.P. Trapper
By Robert Onica

You can tell who he is, by his rough leathery
> fingers,
By his waders, his gloves and slight odor that
> lingers.
Of musky glands, tainted meat, and bottles of lure,
By his traps, chains, and stakes that hold them
> secure.
His face belies years of running his lines,
In the swamps, ponds and meadows, and towering
> pines.
His perils are many, for his harvest he fights
Against weather, the trap thieves, and animal rights.
He braves blizzards, and ice and drifts 10 feet deep,
The land is his life, and he sure earns his keep.
No city man could believe the places he's been,
Or the miracles of nature and marvels he's seen.
A bear in a beehive, a moose cow and calf,
Two fox pups playing, is surely a laugh!
He goes out before dawn, and will stay out past
> dark,
As owls hoot, the wind moans, and coyotes bark.
He reflects on his life, and how hard it may seem.
But deep down inside he knows he's living his
> dream.
If you ask him he'll tell you quite seriously,
You can be a poor trapper, but a rich man in the
> U.P.

A VARIETY OF THOUGHT

Moving to the Upper Peninsula
By R.R. Fretz

Goodbye Detroit, goodbye my friend
Across the Bridge I've gone to spend
Cool summer eves, long winter nights
To revel in leaves and pristine sights
Of field and forest, lake and falls,
A star that chases eerie loon calls.
I'll miss hot jazz and golden arches
No more murders and strike line marches.
A valley sunrise filled with fog
Replaces traffic clogged with smog.
Here people smile preferring to trust,
Bars on windows never a must.
For peace of mind I'm U.P. bound
Days on end with no siren sound.
I walk for miles not seeing a house,
Just deer, beaver, maybe a mouse.
A lone hawk glides above my head
Here in heaven I'll make my bed.
I'll miss my friend, but it's goodbye
My heart rests easy as spirits fly.

YOU AND I
BY CHAS. WHEATLEY

Honor, care, decency.
That's what the U.P.
Means to me.

Beautiful, refreshing to
The soul.

The black knights
Of hatred
haven't befallen
you and I,
Yet.

Flight
By Nancy DeVerna

With upward movement I arise,
To greet the noon day sun.
The brilliant hues of golden rays,
Surround me till I'm warmed.

Below me lie vast crooked snakes,
Of earth-tone browns and grays.
While floating, brilliant greens go by,
And honey colored maze.

The blueness, like an ocean,
Whose horizon never ends.
Engulfs my very being,
Both outwardly and in.

I slowly glide on downward,
Through the rushing of the wind.
To the very ground that I saw from above,
To embrace it once again.

The Pictured Carpet
By P. J. Walsh

There is a Pictured Carpet
Beneath my line of view,
It is the forest tree tops
With many a greenish hue.

I'm in the center of this picture
Way high up in the air,
Looking out upon the scenery
Which is so very calm and fair.

Facing north is Lake Buckeye
With mirrored Pines galore,
And high above this little lake
Two mighty Eagles soar.

With heads and tails the whitest white
And wings spread far and wide,
They make an awe inspiring sight
The emblem of a winning side.

Farther to the distant north
A horizon of waters Blue,
Upon it sailing boats of ore
To see our Country's battles through.

To the northeast lies a logging camp
Upon the Bass Lake shore,
Also Goose and Murray lakes
And rugged hills above the carpet floor.

To Southeast lies a lumbering town
With a background of a hill,

It's name of Newberry, Michigan.
To the right is Dollarville.

Off to the south is Tahquamenon
A deeryard swamp of cedar and spruce,
Also McMillan and Lakefield too
Your home and mine in the County of Luce.

There's Manistique Lakes, all in a line
And farmers fields turning brown,
Even the trees are showing Autumn sign
With whispers of voting in the Hall of our town.

To the Southwest lies Seney
Once the U.P.'s toughest town,
To the Northwest Grand Marais
Where hills and sand dunes on Superior frown.

A Tribute to Mothers
By M. Walsh

America is beautiful and great,
Standing for two hundred years.
This is partly possible through
Our Mothers' prayers and tears.

Yes our Mothers paid for our freedom,
They gave their very best.
Their sons fought so gallantly,
Protecting our rights in the test.

We say "Thank you" dear Mothers.
You have strengthened our nation's back bone.
It's not what you are in the public,
But rather what you are in the home.

The children are their main concern
Whether tiny tot or older.
They love their husbands dearly,
American civilian or soldier.

Some hunt and fish, golf or swim,
Sew and knit, or cook.
Others love to wash and iron,
While others love a good book.

Some Moms are young, still others old,
It's enthusiasm versus experience.
So take the advice of Grandmother
Or you'll pay the consequences.

Some have virtue and good attitudes,
Self-reliance, dignity, and pride.

This can only be accomplished
When peace is reigning inside.

God bless our Moms this special time,
Who have been a blessing to others.
Let's do our best in the month of May
For all of our wonderful Mothers.

The Teacher's Prayer
By M. Walsh

The Lord calls some to the foreign field
With a passion and love for the lost.
They leave their home while heeding the call
Regardless of the cost.

I pray God's blessing upon them daily,
That He guide every step of their life.
As they faithfully give the message clear
In a world full of strife.

I look at myself and then at God's word.
My mission is stated quite clear.
It's not that I travel around the world,
But give the word to those near.

God is not willing that any should perish.
I think of the ones in my class,
Then pray that I'll be faithful always,
Until death unto life they pass.

50th Wedding Anniversary
By M. Walsh

We count it a joy and a privilege
To honor you both this day
Your family, friends and children
Lovisa, Gail, Martin and Jay.

You lived in a cottage by the lake
And over by Hackett's mill
You lived in Flint and Newberry
Now in Lakefield, below the hill.

In years of temptation and trial
And times of loneliness and despair
You always were there when needed
With loving concern and a prayer.

Thanks for the hunting and fishing trips
The picnics and sightseeing at Grand Marais
Picking blueberries, stones and agates
The swimming and cookouts on Helmer Bay.

For who you are and what you've done
We all want to say "Thank you."
A Mom and Dad, friendly and kind
Gracious, thoughtful and true.

To the future please don't worry
America is a beautiful land;
Keep the faith and trust in Him
God holds it in His hand.

There's No Place Like Home
By R. Blanchard

Let me tell you of a place –
Where joy and happiness reign.
A place of golden sunlight,
Where there's never any pain.

Where warm and loving care greet you,
Soon as you enter its door.
A place full of contentment;
Where you know hate is no more.

An environment of comfort;
Where love and friendship are kindled,
A shelter that provides strength.
A place where laughter hasn't dwindled

This place is home!

A Walk in the Woods
By Alice A. Diem

Some walk with their friends,
Some walk with the deer,
Some walk with their dog,
But I walk alone in the woods.

FIE ON YOUR PHOTO
(ON RECEIVING AN UNFLATTERING PICTURE)
BY MARY LOU BAKER

What a blow to my ego
    ("The camera does not lie").
However, 'til my dying day
    I will deny
That I am such a dowdy lump –
    No fulltime total frump
      Am I!

RIDING THE DRYER IN THE LAUNDROMAT
BY LINNEA HENDRICKSON

The laundromat dryer,
round, hard womb,
Sometimes warm.
Climb in! Be a fetus,
Press hard, curl!
Smell the warmth,
Around you go,
Head over heels.
Best ride in town for ten cents.

AGES OLD DILEMMAS

AGES OLD DILEMMAS

The ideas, feelings and experiences expressed in the poems in this section deal with the ages old dilemmas human beings face: Death, disability, war, loss of love, the disappearing of the natural world, poverty. We know that whether we wish it or not, there will be changes in our lives. We can only deal with them as they come and hope that our laments and exhortations will comfort and advise others as well as ourselves. Since the invention of words poetry has been used in this way to honor those who have suffered misfortune, to bewail the tragedies of life and to try to find hope and endurance in words when the realities of living seem to be too much to bear.

Gone Is My Eden
By Katheryn Kunert Bitters

The deer at dusk no longer drink
In rushes by the shore,
The loon's shrill cry no more is heard.

White birches that swayed in the moonlight
Were lost in the rape of the forest.
Oars of flat boats once gently lapped the water.

Now hosts of motor boats rip and roar.
Campers, trailers, vans sending up dust,
Crowds of people sunning on the beach.

Vanished is the quiet –
The solitude no more.
Gone is my Eden.

Submitted by her niece,
Elizabeth Haapalainen

A Gentle Man
By Trish Lasslett

Nearly a generation ago
On a quiet Indian reservation,
Known to all as the White Earth Band,
Was born a manchild
at the time when the season
was gentle, quiet and in rebirth.

As this manchild grew,
he feasted on the fruit of the land.
There was much game cooked by an excellent hand,
to which they added wild rice harvested off the
    land,
followed by berries picked to last all year and
sweetened by the sugar of maple trees.

As this manchild aged
The world was fast changing
The life he knew as a child faded away
But nothing deterred this gentle man.
His love of God and love of family,
made for his stable way of life.

As the girlchild of this gentleman
I am proud to be
For all who knew him came quickly
to recognize his gentle way
A soft laugh, a twinkling eye, a gentle hug.
Ne'er a harsh word spoken.

Wisdom he gained from the Good Book
He applied to his everyway of life.
This gave him a hope of infinite time

to enjoy the grace of God and his family.
He was taken from us unexpectedly,
But he will be remembered by all as . . .

A wise and gentle man,
Who was a friend of God.
My own desire is to follow
in the gentle footsteps of my father
To keep this hope of infinite time
To enjoy the grace of God and family
And to be a friend of God.

Untitled
By Angel Messer

I'm getting over you the only way I can,
I'm getting over you the only way I know.
It's hard to do so I'm taking it slow,
I'm trying hard just to let go.

But life is tough as it's always been
I can't let go till I get to ten.
Ten is miles and miles away,
Until then what do I say?

I could tell you how much I care
But the way you'd treat me is so unfair,
I'd like to have a second try
This time with no goodbyes.

So give US a chance
and, give me a chance to show you,
The love I have for you!!!

Emptiness
By Lori Anne Anderson

Side by side we share the
invisible wall that binds us
to each other in darkened
depths of sadness and uncertainty.

Silence is our shared communication,
and avoidance the sacred, but
frightening resolution to our lives
we live together separately.

Our eyes entranced our souls,
once so familiar and comfortable,
now search longingly for sentiment
when passionate words are none.

I welcomed my lover's embrace completely,
till the emptiness of all emptiness
consumed me totally, and my loneliness
escalated to the depth of once loving him.

Abandoned Fields
By Murray Palmer

It's just a piece of worthless land,
Abandoned, left, divorced from man.
Once fertile fields now grown so poor
That no one here could feel secure.

What fence that's left stands gaunt and grim,
To guard a field there's nothing in,
But weeds and brush, a pile of stone,
The remnants of the farmer's home.

Beneath a gnarled and twisted oak,
A weatherbeaten old ox yoke,
And broken, rusted iron share,
Lie evidence of days of care.

Dark forests frame this saddened scene,
And cast their shadows on the green,
But sparse grown, grass which clothes this soil.
Here someone gave unceasing toil.

Here husbandman worked hard and long,
While in his heart he bore a song.
And on his deep lined leathern face,
He wore a smile, 'twas home, his place.

Where are the sons to claim this land?
Or did they shy from calloused hands?
What mess of pottage was their share
To leave this land without an heir?

PRIORITIES
BY FRANCES ALATALO

Men stand
by the truck
talking about
horses.
The girl and
her horse
are silhouetted
against the
winter landscape's
light dusting
of snow.
Saying goodbye.
"It costs too much
to feed a horse
over winter."
She leads the
horse down,
hands the reins
to the new owner
and walks stiffly
into the house,
not touching the tears
on her face.

A Voice From Within
By Carol Dale Lewis

I see you every day,
you tell me what to do.
I sit alone in my world,
and wish that I were you.

I see you everyday,
as I take your hand.
We take a walk together,
into a different land.

This land is very busy,
its sound is oh so loud.
I want to go back to my world,
away from all the crowds.

I see you every day,
and when it's time to eat
you walk me to my chair,
you make sure I have a seat.

I see you every day,
you get me through the hours,
of simple things like toileting,
and helping me with showers.

I see you every day,
I look forward to your smile.
The love you show me with your time
tells me I'm worthwhile.

So now I want to thank you
because I know you see
no matter how little I can do
there's a person inside of me.

A Quality Of Life
By Lori Anne Anderson

He sat in his wheelchair gurgling ecstatically,
incoherently, happily, as if the best of life
were ultimately here. And I stood smiling
searchingly for happiness amongst the smell
of dried urine and death in gradual process,
unable to feel anything but empathy for him
and guilt because of why I was here.

What? What? I can't understand you.
Patiently, so patiently he tried again,
and again to reach me intellectually,
emotionally, personably. I couldn't
hear. I touched his hand and met his
eye diffidently, timidly, and he gave
me the courage to be his friend.

He sits in his wheelchair gurgling happily,
full of pride in his existence. Life is
here, right now, in this room, in this moment.
(I know not now that tomorrow will be none.)
And I am given the pleasure of sharing
an old man's final hour where the
urine smells of roses.

The War
By Warren Mason

Quiet, the calm before the storm,
Silence, only the people to be warned
Bullets, break the silence of the night,
Fear, the only thought is fright,
The hassle and hustle,
The running to hide,
For the War has come into our sights,
Hysteria, as the bombs come down,
Death, as the bombs hit the ground,
It's over, the War has won,
For the game is lost, and up comes the sun,
For a new day has begun.

Soldier
By Warren Mason

Fear is the only feeling inside
Confronted by my gift of life
Face to face with the meaning of death
I'm glad to be alive, happy with every breath

Fighting for justice and freedom
Just me and my shadow the only one to lean on

Alone in a desert, surrounded by many
but I'm all alone with my thoughts of death
I'm not ready

When suddenly the ultimate fight
Head on with the enemy in my sight
A cold sweat, a feeling of fright
As the bullets break the silence of the night
When it's over no one will know
Except one soldier, with no where to go
For alone now in a coffin for one
For in a war, there is no where to run

Freedom
By P. J. Walsh

They said, We were soft and feeble
    Then, They shot at you and me,
Now we're locked in savage battle
    For the world Supremacy.

We shall always be a people
    In the garden of the free,
If we fight with every pebble,
    For this great Democracy.

The humming wheels of Industry
    Will arm our men in wartime,
Cost is great to keep us free
    And Lumber-Jacks are right in line.

There is no time for dreams today
    In facing great destruction,
We'll lay the axes all away
    With our food in full production.

We must never lose the picture
    In the task we have begun,
For you see it's all because
    Good ole Yankees never run.

We have a weapon mighty strong
    It's our Faith in God above,
With daring courage, one and all
    We'll keep the freedom that we love.

March 13, 1943

Conscious
By P. J. Walsh

Conscious now, we seem to be
Of all good thing in life,
We'll fight our best to keep us free
And weather any strife.

Many tunes are played today
with meanings e'er so deep,
Star Spangled Banner has full sway
And brings us to our feet.

Hats off to Men who've gone so far
Away from ones they love,
They left their homes and pleasure care
A bitter fight they've gone to solve.

No tribute is to great to pay
For men who went on call,
To fight our battles all the way
Their glory surely is too small.

Better days they all will see
With Freedom in their veins,
To build our post-war country
With better Guns, Ships and Planes.

October 15, 1943

Peek-A-Boo Moon
By Trish Lasslett

Peek-a-boo moon
I see you hiding behind the clouds
Don't you know peek-a-boo moon
You can't hide all your light
We know you're there
For God hung you
Long ago with much care
To guide us through
Earth's dark, dark night
So please Peek-a-boo moon
Guide us safely on our way
On this dark, dark night
Come out from behind those clouds
Show us the way
To where we might find safety and light.

Contributors' Biographical Notes

FRANCES ALATALO is a retired psychologist who devotes much of her time to the out-of-doors, gardening and poetry. "This Place" was previously published in *Big Two-Hearted*. "Priorities" was previously published in *The Poetry Peddler*.

LORI ANDERSON is a social worker in her native town of Newberry. Creative writing and reading are hobbies, along with outdoor activities in all seasons.

MARY LOU BAKER grew up in Wisconsin and graduated from the University of Wisconsin. In the U.P. since 1947 and in Newberry since 1950, she has retired from her position as a social worker at the (then) Newberry State Hospital. She is involved in various church and community activities, and is interested in photography, travel, the environment, her family and rockhounding.

KATHERYN KUNERT BITTERS was born and raised in Newberry. She graduated from Newberry High School and University of Michigan, with honors; taught speech, English and history for 25 years in high schools and colleges in Alabama and Ohio, and now resides in a nursing home in Florence, Ala. "Gone Is My Eden" was previously published in *Glowing Embers*, *The Editor's Desk* and *Alura*.

REBECCA BLANCHARD was born in 1977. She likes writing stories and poems in her spare time. She also enjoys reading, ice skating, playing the piano, and school in Newberry.

NANCY DEVERNA, originally from Lambertville, Mich., moved to McMillan in 1980. She graduated from Bedford Public Schools and Northern Michigan University. She and her husband have two grown children, both graduates of Tahquamenon Area Schools.

ALICE DIEM was born in 1977 and attends school in Grosse Pointe Woods, Mich. She summers on Sprang's Point near Curtis, Mich.

BILL DIEM graduated from Ohio Wesleyan University. He has vacationed in or near Curtis since 1954, and with his wife, Mary, purchased the Newberry News in 1989 from William and Avis Fretz.

RANDALL FRETZ moved to the U.P. in 1990 after visiting for more than 30 years. A former reporter and sports editor of a downstate weekly, Randy is a teacher at Newberry who enjoys many outdoor activities.

MARGARET JORDAN FURLONG (1896-1985) was a resident of Newberry from 1936 until her death. She was very active in civic affairs.

FRANK GORDON is a retired school teacher and athletic coach. He graduated from Wittenberg College in Springfield, Ohio, and operated Gordon's Resort in Curtis from 1947 until 1989. He lives in Curtis with his wife, Lillian.

SAVILLA HANDRICH and her husband, Bruce, moved to Germfask in 1947 and have lived there except for one year spent in Prescott, Ariz. Their eight children are spread across the U.S. She has spent quite a few years in restaurant work; special interests are quilting and gardening.

LINNEA HENDRICKSON was a child in Newberry and worked several summers at the Falls. She now lives in Albuquerque, N.M., with her husband and two children. She is the author of *Children's Literature: A Guide to Criticism*, and she sometimes teaches children's literature. Despite living in Australia and elsewhere: "No matter how many wonderful places I have visited and lived in, the U.P. remains my true home."

CAROL JENKINS was born in Detroit in 1934, and moved to Brevort Dec. 15, 1969. She is the mother of six children and four step-children and grandmother of five. A lover of nature, her hobbies are writing, photography, art, swimming and cross country skiing. She enjoys music, friends, animals and all of God's creations.

BILL KOLASINSKI moved to the U.P. in 1968 with his wife, Lucy, to take over operation of Camp Chick-a-Gamee on South Manistique Lake. Their sons Gypsy and Sunshine are graduates of Newberry High School.

TRISH LASSLETT is a Native American who has lived in Newberry with her husband and four children since 1972. She works as a bookkeeper.

JOHN E. LEE
I was born in Jackson Mich. in the year of '35.
I moved all over the country in an effort to stay alive.
On the east coast and the west coast, these places I have been.
But there is no place like Newberry! I know I'm home again.

CAROL DALE LEWIS grew up in North Rudyard. She is happily married with five children and has worked with the elderly and the developmentally disabled. "I have seen through their eyes that everyone is an individual and that everyone has worth. I dedicate 'A Voice from Within' to all persons who are unable to care for themselves for whatever reason and to all who work with such individuals."

WARREN MASON, born in the mid-'70s in Sault Ste. Marie, now lives in Eastchester, N.Y., but he continues to visit the U.P. often. In his spare time he enjoys hanging out with friends and listening to music. He lives by the motto: "To be excellent one must practice excellence."

ANGEL MESSER has lived in Newberry and Houghton.

BILLIE J. OBEY was born in Newberry during the Depression and grew up with the whistles. After graduation she married and with her family has enjoyed the outdoor activities of this area. Since retirement from the Mental Health Center after 28 years, she has time to travel, pursue hobbies and putter in her flower garden.

ROBERT D. ONICA, born in the late 1950s, is an ex-Marine employed by the Postal Service in Pontiac, Mich. He lives in Keego Harbor, Mich., but owns a year-round home near Newberry that he and his wife visit frequently. Besides hunting, fishing and trapping, he enjoys performing as a professional magician.

MURRAY PALMER, of McMillan, started writing poetry as a teenager and has continued through college and his retirement as a psychiatric nurse administrator at the Newberry Regional Mental Health Center. Now engaged in theology study, he still finds time for a poem or two. "Abandoned Fields" and "The Birth of Spring" were previously published in *The Communicator*.

N. JUNE PEAKE was born and raised in the Strongs-Eckerman-Hulbert area. She graduated from Hulbert High School and attended Ferris Institute. She and her husband, Roger, moved to Arlington Heights, Ill., in 1985, and plan to return to Hulbert to build their retirement home. Their son Leon is career Navy. She enjoys visiting with her grandchildren, traveling and writing poetry and fiction.

BEVERLY and ROBERT SCHAEFER are returned natives of the U.P. They taught school in Jackson, Mich., and are now retired. They spent summers at their campground on North Manistique Lake for 27 years.

DR. PETER SCHAEFER is the son of Beverly and Robert. He is in forestry research at a university in South Dakota.

LT. RICHARD SCHAEFER is another son of Beverly and Robert. He is in the Coast Guard, stationed in Washington, D.C. Like his brother Peter, he visits his parents often.

OSCAR J. SUNDSTROM was born, raised and educated in Newberry, leaving there for college and military draft prior to World War II. He also served in Korea and Vietnam, retiring from the Air Force after 31 years with the rank of Colonel. As a youngster he did odd jobs, worked in the mill, as a grocery and clothing store clerk, in construction and as a news reporter when he was not running a teenage trap line.

CHARLES SPRAGUE TAYLOR (1920-1976). From his boyhood, Sprague Taylor was fascinated by forests, streams and the early history of what he called "our neck of the woods." This interest continued during years as timber producer and sawmill operator. His research and photography collection has remained a valued resource in the community, With the exception of a few years spent away in school and Army service, he spent his life in the area, at Hulbert, Eckerman, Strongs and Newberry.

D.J. WALSH was raised in Lakefield Township, McMillan. He and his wife have served as missionaries in Bangladesh for 31 years.

MARTIN WALSH was born in Lakefield and has lived in Newberry all his life. He is retired from the Mental Health Center after 31 years. He is an avid hunter and fisherman.

P.J. WALSH was born at Mayfield, Grand Traverse County, June 23, 1910. He came to Luce County in 1930. He worked at different jobs and retired from the Department of Conservation after 25 years.

CHARLES WHEATLEY was born in New York City in 1940. He served three years overseas in the U.S. Army. He has worked in many shops and factories in the Detroit area as a machine operator and has lived in the U.P. for four years.

INDEX

FRANCES ALATALO	23, 28, 39, 41, 90
LORI ANDERSON	16, 20, 49, 88, 92
MARY LOU BAKER	45, 81
KATHERYN KUNERT BITTERS	84
REBECCA BLANCHARD	80
NANCY DEVERNA	73
ALICE DIEM	80
BILL DIEM	56
RANDALL FRETZ	15, 71
MARGARET JORDAN FURLONG	31
FRANK GORDON	63, 64, 65
SAVILLA HANDRICH	27
LINNEA HENDRICKSON	38, 81
CAROL JENKINS	46
TRISH LASSLETT	12, 43, 85, 97
JOHN E. LEE	21, 67
CAROL DALE LEWIS	91
WARREN MASON	93, 94
ANGEL MESSER	87
BILLIE J. OBEY	2
ROBERT D. ONICA	68
MURRAY PALMER	7, 30, 44, 89
N. JUNE PEAKE	8, 17, 18, 24, 32, 34, 48, 62
BEVERLY SCHAEFER	14
ROBERT SCHAEFER	13, 51, 60
DR. PETER SCHAEFER	19
LT. RICHARD SCHAEFER	19
OSCAR J. SUNDSTROM	4, 5, 6, 22
CHARLES SPRAGUE TAYLOR	33
D. J. WALSH	58
MARTIN WALSH	66, 76, 78, 79
P. J. WALSH	25, 50, 74, 95, 96
CHARLES WHEATLEY	72